Scriptural Prayers for America & Donald Trump

★ For This Critical Time In History ★

Karen Hardin

Scriptural Prayers For America & Donald Trump
ISBN 979-8-9888420-2-6
Copyright © 2024 by Karen Hardin
P. O. Box 700515
Tulsa, OK 74170

Scripture quotations are patterned from the *Holy Bible, New International Version*®. Copyright © 1973, 1978, 1984, 2011 by Biblica, Inc.® Used by permission. All rights reserved worldwide.

Published by Paladin Publishing
Represented by PriorityPR Group & Literary Agency.
www.prioritypr.org

Photo credit: Natilyn Photography — Unsplash
Text Design: Lisa Simpson

Printed in the United States. All rights reserved under International Copyright Law. No part of this publication may be reproduced, stored in a retrieval system, or transmitted in any form or by any means—electronic, mechanical, photocopy, recording, or any other—except for brief quotations in printed reviews, without prior permission of the publisher.

"Never doubt that a small group of thoughtful, committed citizens can change the world; indeed, it's the only thing that ever has."[1]

*Margaret Mead
(American cultural anthropologist)*

"Prayer honors God, acknowledges His being, exalts His power, adores His providence, secures His aid."[2]

E.M. Bounds

Contents

Introduction 7
Where Has Justice Gone? 11
Noontime Corporate Prayer 17
Prayer for Liberty 23
Prayer for Donald J. Trump 27
Vindication & Justice For Donald J. Trump 31
Protection Over Donald Trump and Family 36
Restoration of DJT Finances & Businesses 40
Restoration of Our Legal System 43
Restoration of Our Government
   & Trust In It 46
Restoration of Law and Order 52
Election Integrity & Upcoming Election(s) 57
Prayer Over Elected Officials 67
Coup Creators & Stolen Seats 74
Regarding the National Debt 80
For Righteous Judges 83
The Media 87
Freedom of Speech 93

Exposure of Corruption 96
Truth Regarding 2020 Election &
    Protection Over Upcoming Elections 100
Release of Political Prisoners............................ 106
Prayers For America to Wake Up! 112
Courage For Americans to Stand 118
Protection From Violence and Intimidation... 122
America to Be Restored.................................... 126
Our Prophetic Declaration Over America 130
Can America Be Saved? 136
City by City... 141
Destiny Builders 142
Endnotes 143

INTRODUCTION

I wrote these prayers as "we" rather than "I" intentionally to represent collective corporate prayer. Each time these prayers are prayed, whether across America or across the world, we unite asking God, Our Creator, to hear our cry for our nation and for Donald Trump.

Like him or not, it is hard to deny the animosity that has arisen against Donald Trump. The Trump Derangement Syndrome is real and those infected by it are determined to remove and destroy him. Not only from the possibility of running for office, but according to some, from existence.

Consider some of the following statements publicly made against him:

- Representative Dan Goldman (NY-D) recently called for Trump to be "eliminated."[3]

- "The View" talk show co-host, Joy Behar, called him a "domestic terrorist."[4]

- "The View" talk show co-host, Whoopi Goldberg taunted Donald Trump's comment that he would run for office in 2024 saying, "You're not going to run if you're in jail" projecting the obvious goal of those frantic to keep him out of office.[5]

- Or remember when Madonna proclaimed to a crowd of thousands at the Women's March on Washington in January 2017 that she had "thought an awful lot about blowing up the White House."[6]

Introduction

- Or when comedian Kathy Griffin held up a what looked to be a bloodied decapitated head of then—President Donald Trump.

What about the current judge presiding over the New York legal case? Judge Arthur Engoron, single-handedly denied Trump his constitutional right of "innocent until proven guilty" when he entered summary judgment against the defendant before the trial even began[7]. Additionally, Engoron has repeatedly refused to let Trump respond fully to questions asked saying, "I'm not here to hear what he has to say. He's here to answer questions."[8] But then the judge doesn't let him.

Never have we seen such animosity and denial of justice as we currently see against this man and those who support him.

I am not a "Trumper." But it isn't hard to see there is only one candidate that those wishing to destroy America fear—Donald Trump. That should tell us everything we need to know about who to support to oppose their ongoing attempt to take over America and destroy freedom.

The prayers that follow are predominantly from scripture written in prayer form. The scripture references used are at the bottom of each page.

WHERE HAS JUSTICE GONE?

*"Each time a man stands up for an ideal
or acts to improve the lot of others or
strikes out against injustice,
he sends forth a tiny
ripple of hope."*
—*Robert Kennedy*

Where has justice gone? The corruption of America's judicial system, three-letter agencies such as the FBI and CIA, and those currently occupying the White House, has never been more evident. Especially over the last few years, we have watched as good men have been found guilty and/or sentenced to prison while corrupt leaders, with clear evidence of illegal actions, have been given a pass.

We now live in a nation where evidence, that could exonerate individuals, is hidden—kept from the public and from the courtroom. Where committees are created to "investigate," but some have only manipulated and released information to support the narrative of their predetermined verdict.

Consider the final report from the J6 Committee. It was made up of nine self-avowed Trump-hating Congressional members, who submitted eight chapters of their investigation into the Trump family rather than a full investigation into what really happened on January 6, 2021.

Where was the investigation into Nancy Pelosi? Washington, D.C. Mayor Muriel Bowser? Or their combined efforts to reduce the number of Capitol police on duty that day? What about their refusal to approve the request for National Guardsmen from Donald Trump?

What about the media's continued portrayal of that day as "Trump's attempt to overthrow the 2020 election?" Rather than what it really was which was the attempt to investigate the irregularities of the 2020 election? The certification of the electoral votes, which took place that day, should have been delayed for an investigation into the mounting evidence of fraud. Instead, those who posted first-person accounts and video of election fraud were censored.

Where has justice gone?

What about the FBI agent instigators dressed as Trump supporters who were working the crowd that day and even in the Capitol?

Why were thousands of hours of video from inside the Capitol Building from January 6 kept from defense lawyers of those arrested and kept from the public? It was only after Republican Speaker of the House, Mike Johnson, was elected three years later, that it was finally released so the American people could see the truth. What about the J6 investigative committee that hid the truth? Will there be any reprisal for their one-sided "investigation"?

Where has justice gone?

Why was Donald Trump's home raided by the FBI for alleged mishandling of classified documents[10], (which as president he could declassify) but when Joe Biden was found in possession of classified documents at one of his homes and three other locations (and he had no such authority as a then-senator to possess those documents) his home was not raided, no charges were filed and no ongoing investigation seems to be taking place.

Where has justice gone?

Why is Donald Trump on trial before a judge who already submitted a summary judgment of guilt before the trial began? How can a trial be fair when that same judge has said I'm not here to listen to what Donald Trump has to say? What is he there for, if not to listen impartially to all the evidence and then make a decision?

How is a judge allowed to issue a gag order not only on the president but on his lawyers, so they can't even make an objection in court?

Since when does an attorney general or a lawyer become an authority on land appraisal value to make a self-determination that Donald Trump was guilty of overvaluing his property? Why were they able to determine a value without following the procedure for land appraisal which would be the evaluation of comparable properties in the same area?

Where has justice gone?

This book is an urgent call to prayer for the restoration of justice, not only for Donald Trump, but also, fair elections and protection of liberty for America and all American citizens.

We must not only pray against injustice but be willing to speak out against it and take a stand. For as we do, we send forth that tiny ripple of hope. We empower others to have courage.

Will you join me?

NOONTIME CORPORATE PRAYER

For America and Donald Trump

Father, we come before you united together in prayer on behalf of America and Donald Trump. You said that where two or three are gathered together in Your name that You will be in our midst. We invite Your Presence and power as we pray that You would hear our cry for justice and truth to be restored to this land You love.

We lift up Donald Trump and his family. Where there has been ongoing accusations, lawsuits and injustice thrown at him, we pray for America's justice system to be restored. We declare unrighteous judges to be removed and held accountable for refusing to follow the law or creating their own. Where they have worked to silence him and his legal team, we pray that it would come back on them. May they be the ones silenced and removed from their positions as they have tried to remove him. We ask that You would raise up judges, as in the days of old, who will deliver righteous decrees. Deliver Donald Trump from the hands of those intent on plundering his businesses and wealth with unjust indictments.

In You, O LORD, we take refuge; let us never be put to shame. We ask that You would save Donald Trump and America by Your righteousness. Incline Your ear to our cry for help; come quickly to his and our rescue. Be his rock of refuge, the stronghold of his deliverance from their determination to find him guilty and prevent him from running for office. They are coming at him (and us) at every side. We don't know what to do, but our eyes are on You.

We hear their slander and there is terror on every side. They conspire against him and plot to take his life. We pray for supernatural protection over him and his family. We pray they would put their trust in You as we do, O LORD; and say, "You are my God." Our times are in Your hands; deliver us from our enemies and from those who pursue him. Make Your face shine upon him; save him from their evil plans by Your loving kindness.

Where judges have overstepped their authority to override what professional appraisers and banks have declared the value of his properties in their effort to bankrupt him, we declare their efforts null and void. Where they have worked to diminish his wealth, we pray supernatural blessing over it and that You would restore seven-fold what has been stolen. We declare Your protection over the paths of justice that You would guard the way of those who are loyal to You.

We bind every harassing, deceptive spirit that is operating against Donald Trump and our nation. We pray that the trap they have laid they will fall into themselves. Let the light overtake and expose what they have done in the the dark.

Lord we ask that You would not remain silent regarding this issue. For the wicked and the deceitful have opened their mouths against Donald Trump, and against those who have stood with him for truth. Many have worked relentlessly to destroy this nation that You love. Contend with those who contend with us and fight against those who fight against us. Come to our aid and deliver us from evil.

Honest scales and balances belong to You LORD for all the weights in the bag are of Your making. And so we declare that honesty and fairness will be restored to America's justice system and with it the removal of corrupt leaders, officials, law-enforcement, judges and lawyers who have worked to pervert justice and who have declared evil good and good evil.

Our nation was founded on godly principles and we declare it will be restored to those principles and the Constitution on which it was established. John Adams stated "Our Constitution was made only for a moral and religious people. It is wholly inadequate to the government of any other." That explains why they hate it. So hear our cry this day, O Lord, as we humble ourselves before You and ask You to heal our land. We repent for the degradation that has taken place on our watch and ask that You turn America back to a moral people whose hearts fear and honor You.

Who will once again see the blessing and miracle of America and our Constitution. We pray a hedge of protection around it that despite their best efforts that they will be the ones overthrown in their attempt to overthrow it.

Matt 18:20, Judges 2:16, Ps 31:1-2 & 13-17, 2 Chron 20:12, Prov 6;31, Prov 2:8, Ps 35:1 & 8, Prov 16:11, Is 5:20, 2 Chron 7:14

PRAYER FOR LIBERTY

"He who would trade liberty for some temporary security, deserves neither liberty nor security."
—Benjamin Franklin

Father, we call upon Your name and thank You that You hear us when we call. It is for freedom that You have set us free from the power of sin. Even now we ask that You would set us free from those who desire to enslave us to a yoke of tyranny. We stand firm, then, spiritually and physically that we be not burdened again by a yoke of slavery in either area. We call on Your name Lord for help.

We have traded liberty for the promise of safety. Yet we have been lied to and deceived and given away much of the precious hard-earned freedom gained at America's birth.

Hear our cry O Lord and deliver us from those intent on destroying this nation and stealing the liberty and freedom upon which America was established. Forgive us that we have taken it for granted and that we have remained silent and did nothing to circumvent this evil. We repent—and we ask now for Your help.

We thank you for America and for the Constitution written to protect these freedoms. May it remain strong and unchanged from the hands of those who wish to destroy it. We thank you for those before us who gave their very lives so that we could be free. May we not lose that freedom now.

We can belatedly see that America is on the same road as other countries before us who were stripped of their liberty and wealth as communism tries to infiltrate our government. Those who have lived through such atrocity have warned us and yet the minds of many have been captured to believe our land and forefathers were evil. Open the eyes of the citizens of this nation, both young and old, to know the truth.

We know that Your hand has been on this nation and we ask for Your divine guidance for reformation and restoration of our rights and liberty which have slowly been relinquished for the promise of safety—a lie which they have no intention of fulfilling. Forgive us.

It has been said that "People have only as much liberty as they have the intelligence to want and the courage to take."[11] Give us both intelligence and courage to take back this land and maintain our freedom.

Let all who take refuge in You be glad. Let us ever sing for joy. Spread Your protection over us, that those who love Your name may rejoice in You. For surely, Lord, You said You would bless the righteous; and surround us with Your favor as with a shield. We know that You will maintain the cause of the afflicted and help us Lord. We declare that justice and truth will return as will the fear of the Lord.

Gal 5:1, Ps 5:11-12, Ps 140:12

Prayer for Donald J. Trump

"It was pride that changed angels into devils; it is humility that makes men as angels."[12]

—*Saint Augustine*

We ask You to draw Donald Trump into an intimate relationship with You. Your Word says the heart of the king is in Your hand and You turn it wherever You please. We pray this day, that his heart would be set upon You. Fill him with Your wisdom. Give him strength so that he will run and not be weary and walk and not faint.

We pray that he would exchange any area where there has been pride for a spirit of humility. For You oppose the proud but give grace to the humble. Pour out Your grace and favor upon him as he seeks You.

Anoint him with the power of the Holy Spirit, that he would feel You with him everywhere he goes. May his steps be ordered and directed by You. We ask You to strengthen him in the inner man and that he would walk daily in the strength of the Lord.

Father, we ask You to visit him in the night hours. Give him dreams and visions, and divine visitations. May he put his trust completely in You. Whether he turns to the right or to the left, may he hear the voice of the Holy Spirit behind him, saying, "This is the way; walk in it." We command confusion, pride, and/or fear to go. In the midst of this attack, we pray he would turn to the name of the Lord as his strong tower.

May integrity and humility guide every decision he makes. Turn his heart from all distractions and cause him to look to You for help and insight. You said in the multitude of counselors there is safety. Surround him with godly counsel. We also pray that any who give wrong and/or ungodly counsel would be removed. Give him discernment to know who to trust and who to listen to. You said that victory is won through many advisors. We declare Donald Trump is surrounded with godly advisors and supernatural victory against the attempts to silence him, imprison him and destroy him.

May he serve You as a true leader, with wisdom, insight, endless hope and unwavering faith. May the enemies that have risen against him one way, flee before him seven.

We declare this day that You go before him and make every crooked place straight. Gird him daily with strength and make his way perfect. Thank You for keeping him firmly hidden in the shelter of Your wings.

Prov 21:1, Is 41:10, James 4:6, Ps 37:23, Eph 3:16, Prov 18:10, Is 30:21, Prov 11:14, Prov 24:6, Deut 28:7, Is 45:2, Ps 18:32, Ps 91:4

VINDICATION & JUSTICE FOR DONALD J. TRUMP

"Justice delayed is justice denied."
—William E. Gladstone

𝓛ord, You said that what we bind on earth is bound in heaven and what we loose on earth will be loosed in heaven. Today we bind the lies streaming from the media, and all those intent on silencing and removing Donald J. Trump. We declare that the trap they have laid they will fall into themselves.

Where they have tried to silence him, may they be silenced.

Where they have declared him guilty of the very things they have done, may their judgment of him become their judgment. For by the words of their mouth they will be snared.

Where he has had unjust fines and penalties leveled against him, may those who pronounced those fines and penalties have to pay him restitution.

We declare the boulder they have rolled down against him, will crush them instead. We bind the lying spirits and in their place we loose the spirit of truth.

Father, You said no weapon formed against us would prosper and that we would refute every tongue that accuses us. In Jesus's name, we refute the lies of the media, judges, elected officials, etc. who have used their positions to spread the false as fact and call for their mouths to be shut just as you closed the mouths of the lions in Daniel's day.

Lord, we ask that you would not only silence the lying lips which speak arrogantly against the righteous with pride and contempt, but you would hide Donald Trump in a secret shelter from the strife of tongues—which means contentions divisions and lawsuits.

Expose the lies. You said that whoever pours out lies will not go free. Expose where there have been unjust judgments and statements made that disavow the truth and ignore the facts.

Lord we ask for justice and righteousness to prevail. Hold the unrighteous accountable for the lies that they spew. Who have used their positions to try to remove him from office or prevent him from running for office.

Vindicate Donald Trump as well as those who have been falsely accused, imprisoned, or fined as they have stood with him for justice and righteousness for our nation. For this is the heritage of the servants of the Lord and our vindication is from You.

You said you would contend with those who contend with us and You would fight against those who fight against us. Lord, we ask for You to show up and bring Your vindication in this hour against this evil.

We declare that although they plot against him and against us, their evil schemes will not succeed.

We declare that the justice due us does not escape your notice for You are the Everlasting God, the Lord the Creator of the ends of the earth. You do not become weary or tired and Your understanding is inscrutable. You give strength to the weary and to him who lacks might You increase power. Though youths grow weary and tired and vigorous young men stumble badly, yet You said *all* who wait on You will gain new strength. Lord re-energize

Donald Trump and his family, his lawyers and the citizens who are fighting for the protection of this nation so we will not give up but continue to press in until we see the salvation of the Lord.

May Your glory be revealed in our nation and throughout the world that all will see that YOU are Lord over America and Your hand is upon us for a just outcome. Our hope and trust are in You.

Matt 18:18, Prov 26:27, Prov 6:2, Is 54:17, Ps. 31:18,19, Ps. 35: 1, Prov 19:5, Ps 21:11, Is 40:27-31

Protection Over Donald Trump and Family

"Every good citizen makes his country's honor his own, and cherishes it not only as precious but as sacred. He is willing to risk his life in its defense and its conscious that he gains protection while he gives it."[13]

—Andrew Jackson

We plead the blood of Jesus over Donald Trump and his family. We ask You to keep them safe from all harm. We declare no bullet, knife, poison, bomb, assassination attempt of any kind or verbal onslaught can touch them. Just as they tried to kill George Washington in battle[14], but could not, so may it be for Donald Trump and his family. We declare any attempt to kill them would fail.

Anoint them to stand firm in this season, in peace and in Your Presence.

We pray they will not fear, for You are with them. That they will not be dismayed, for You are their God. Strengthen them and help them in this hour of need. Uphold them with Your righteous right hand.

We declare Your faithfulness like a shield and a protective wall around them so they do not need to fear the terror of night, or the arrow that flies by day.

We declare they are strong in the Lord and in the power of Your might. As they stand fast in this battle may they be careful to obey You and Your laws. Grant them success wherever they go.

In You, Lord, may they take refuge. Let them never be put to shame. Deliver them in Your righteousness. As they turn their ear to You, we pray You would go quickly to their rescue. Be their rock of refuge and a strong fortress to save them from the battle and violence against them. Since You are their rock and fortress, for the sake of Your name lead and guide them so that the world will see and know it is You protecting them and delivering them. Keep them free from the trap that has been set for them. For You are their refuge.

May this Book of the Law always be on their lips. May they meditate on it day and night, so that they will be careful to do everything written in it. Then they will be prosperous and have good success. Make them strong, courageous and unafraid. We command discouragement and weariness to go.

May the peace of God that passes all understanding keep their hearts and minds in Christ Jesus. Keep them in perfect peace as their mind is steadfast on You.

We put You in remembrance of Your Word that You said You will rescue and protect us as we acknowledge You. You said when we call on You, You will answer us. That You would be with us in trouble to deliver us and honor us and satisfy us with long life and show us Your salvation.

We ask You for that protection and deliverance for Donald Trump and his family. Vindicate them. Show them Your saving hand. We put our trust in You Lord and stand fast that You are in control and will show Yourself strong.

Is 41:10-11, Ps 91:4-6, Ps 20:4, Ps 18:2, Joshua 1:8, Phil 4:7, Is 26:3, Ps 91:15-16, Ps 43:1

Restoration of DJT Finances & Businesses

A society that robs an individual of the product of his effort, or enslaves him, or attempts to limit the freedom of his mind, or compels him to act against his own rational judgment ... is not, strictly speaking, a society, but a mob held together by institutionalized gang-rule.[15]

—Ayn Rand

Father, where Donald Trump refused to take his salary when he served as president, we ask that You would multiply his gift as an offering unto You. We ask that You would multiply him a thousand times over and bless him for the personal sacrifices he has made of his time, money and businesses to help restore this nation.

You said when the thief is caught, he must pay back sevenfold. We pray where the judges have imposed fines against his businesses and against him personally, that they would be "caught" and that there would be a sevenfold restoration of that which has been stolen. We declare restitution over any theft or devaluation of his properties, his businesses and his home.

Where they have unjustly surveilled him, raided his home, penalized him, or indicted him on false premises, we ask that You would restore to him that which has been taken from his peace of mind, wealth and the ability to conduct business.

Restore all that has been stolen. Grant him favor. As he follows after You, open for him the good treasure house, the heavens, to give him rain for his land in its season and to bless all he does. That he will lend to many nations but borrow from none.

We pray as he leads this nation, for that same blessing to be restored on America that we would no longer be a debtor nation, but a lender.

Where there have been those who have "ridden over his head," where he has gone through fire and water, we declare the end result will be that You bring him out to a place of abundance.

Deut 1:11, Prov 6:31, Deut 28:12, Ps 66:12

RESTORATION OF OUR LEGAL SYSTEM

"Justice will not be served until those who are unaffected are as outraged as those who are."

—often attributed to Benjamin Franklin

𝓕ather, our legal system has become a mockery of thievery, bribery, and extortion. Where the innocent are found guilty and the guilty face no consequences for their crimes and illegal activities.

It has become a system that we no longer trust. We pray for the restoration of the fear of the Lord within it and those who are part of it, for only then can we see a return to wisdom and fairness.

We declare, "Woe to those who call evil good and good evil, who put darkness for light and light for darkness, who are wise in their own eyes and clever in their own sight." May their corruption and illegalities done in secret be brought into the light.

Where justice has been denied and our legal system exploited, we pray that the loopholes in the law, which have allowed evil to continue, be found, closed and stopped.

You see and know those who have foolishly said, "There is no God." Those who are corrupt, and their deeds vile and who have no remorse for their actions. We pray that their legal license, or their position within our legal system be removed so that they can no longer corrupt the system.

You alone sit as Judge over all the peoples of the earth and we ask that You would expose the injustice and restore our legal system to once again follow just laws. For You detest dishonest scales, but accurate weights find favor with You.

You warned that if we fail under pressure our strength is too small. May we not fail in this endeavor to pray and see our legal system restored. We want to see our nation turn back to You, but how can we do that when corrupt legislators and/or lawyers and unrighteous judges continue to make or interpret laws and rulings on behalf of criminals?

But let justice roll on like a river and truth and righteousness like a never-failing stream! Be the stability of our times of our legal system. A wealth of salvation, wisdom and knowledge where the fear of the Lord is our treasure.

Ps 111:10, Is 5:20-21, Luke 8:17, Ps 14:1, Prov 11:1, Prov 24:10, Amos 5:24, Is 33:6

Restoration of Our Government & Trust In It

Government is merely a servant – merely a temporary servant; it cannot be its prerogative to determine what is right and what is wrong, and decide who is a patriot and who isn't. Its function is to obey orders, not originate them.[16]

—*Mark Twain*

Father, we pray for all of America's government—federal, state, county, and city levels. First of all, we make supplication, intercession and give thanks for those who serve in those positions and all who are in authority over us, so that we can lead a quiet and peaceful life in all godliness and reverence. For those who serve with integrity and honor, we pray Your blessing upon them. For those who serve for their own gain and power, we pray that their hearts would be turned back to You and that they would serve the people rather than themselves.

Many have worked to deceive Americans into believing the fallacious argument of "separation and church and state." Many now believe it is in the Constitution and/or a law of the land when it is neither. May the truth overtake the lie. We pray that Americans would wake up and recognize the lie, which is in complete contradiction to our Constitution and American history.

We thank you for the remarkable U.S. Constitution on which our government stands. Woven into its very fabric is scripture and the firm belief and honor of You. May that never be stolen from us. We thank you that the laws of our Constitution provide a climate in which the gospel can be preached effectively. We declare that right will also not be stolen. We ask for protection over this guiding document of our nation that it will not be dismantled, thrown out or rewritten as they are trying to do now.

We pray for a good government with the characteristics to·maintain law and order, promote a sound infrastructure, transparent and honest communication, preserve civil liberty, protect our freedom of speech, freedom of assembly and the freedoms outlined in the Bill of Rights.

We declare where bad government has been established creating a break-down of law and order permitting lawlessness, unsafe conditions for citizens, censorship of truth, intentional destruction of our infrastructure and economy, unjust and arbitrary restrictions against rightful citizens giving away our freedom, wealth and privileges as citizens to those who are not, we pray that those who are instituting these policies would be removed, cast out and brought to justice. They do not represent Americans nor do they desire to protect our nation.

We repent where we mistakenly voted some of them into office. For those we didn't, we pray that we are not held accountable for the decisions they have made to take our nation down a road we do not condone.

We declare the penalty of their actions, against You and the American people, to fall on their own heads. Hold them, not us, accountable for the despicable, sinful acts they have committed to change our government and laws that are contrary to our beliefs and against righteousness.

Where our government has enacted policy and made requests that has forced

Israel to give up land and safety, we repent. May our government remain a close ally of Israel as we pray for her protection and the peace of Jerusalem.

Deliver us from the tyrannical government that has formed and for those who seek to destroy our nation and our freedom.

We pray for a good government, along with good leaders who will fear and honor You and serve the people. We pray they will hear and follow Your voice.

Where they have instituted oppressive decrees, deprived us of our rights and withheld justice and oppressed us, we ask that You would intervene on our behalf and rescue us from perverse and evil men. You said You would deliver us from the hand of the wicked and will redeem us from the grasp of the violent.

Lord, remove those who have abused their positions and their authority. We pray that they will be brought to justice as their illegal actions are exposed. We declare that the weaponization of our government will come to an end and that it will once again function as it was created to function—to serve the people.

Make a distinction between the righteous and the wicked. Between the ones who serve You and those who don't. Lord, we watch and wait expectantly for You, the God of our salvation. May Your glory be revealed as we pray for our nation to turn back to You and the destiny upon which she was established.

1 Timothy 2:1-2, Is 9:6, Ps 122:6, 2 Thes 3:2, Jer 15:21, Malachi 3:18, Micah 7:7, Micah 6:4

RESTORATION OF LAW AND ORDER

"Law and order exist for the purpose of establishing justice and when they fail in this purpose they become the dangerously structured dams that block the flow of social progress."[17]

—*Martin Luther King, Jr.*

Father, we pray over police officers, sheriffs, deputies, all law enforcement, and first responders. Thank You for Your angels that are encamped round about them. Keep them safe from harm, attack, accidents, or discouragement. We pray they would know that they are valuable and valued and the shame that some have tried to place on those who serve in this capacity would be uprooted and removed.

We pray for law enforcement and first responders, who sacrifice much and put their lives on the line each day. We pray they would be compensated well for their service. Where cities and/or states have tried to defund them, we pray for a reversal of those actions so that the citizens and our nation would be protected.

Where law enforcement officers have had to worry about legal action taken against them when they do their jobs, we pray that they will be protected from unjust lawsuits and retribution. We pray that You would give them supernatural discernment in each situation they encounter where they have to or need to use deadly force so that it is only when essential. May that authority never be abused.

Where there are cities in which law enforcement has been overwhelmed by lawlessness, we pray that those who have tried to tie their hands from being able to perform their duties be removed. May the laws that have been instituted specifically to increase lawlessness, and where it has made people's love grow cold, let there be a reversal so that lawlessness will be cast down along with those who have enabled it.

We pray for those in law enforcement who have given the profession a bad name and who have operated without integrity or honor. For those who are corrupt, who have taken bribes, who stir division, who misuse and abuse their authority, who laugh at the down-trodden, who align with and help thieves or kowtow to them, Lord may they repent, change and become officers of integrity, or be removed and exposed now. We know they are not the majority and have given all law enforcement a bad name. We pray corruption in all areas of law enforcement be exposed and stopped and ask that You would restore trust and the good name of those who entered this profession with the deep desire to help and protect.

We also pray for the families of those in law enforcement and first responders. We pray peace for their hearts and minds, protection and blessing upon them both financially, emotionally and physically for the sacrifices made of those serving along with their families. Bless them and protect them Lord.

We pray that those who have devised destructive plans, attacks and harm against our law enforcement officers and first responders, may their evil plans be discovered before they can be launched and fail. We pray that America will not be overrun by lawlessness, but be restored as a nation that has the fear of the Lord and respect for the law.

> Ps 34:7, Matt 24:12

ELECTION INTEGRITY & UPCOMING ELECTION(S)

"In the absence of justice, what is sovereignty but organized robbery?"[18]

—*Saint Augustine*

Father, we pray on behalf of our nation and our elections. Thank You that we have the right to vote. May it never be taken from us. We declare our elections will be honest and fair. Help us hold this privilege and responsibility as a sacred duty.

We plead the blood of Jesus over the entire process. We ask You to deploy warring angels to stand post at every polling location and every election board. That they will stop any vote tampering or illegalities.

We declare all nefarious plans that would try to subvert a fair election process be thwarted. May those who devise wicked plans along with those who are false witnesses who speak lies, face the consequences of their actions and fail in their attempt to deceive and change the true outcome of our elections. We declare no weapon formed against our elections will prosper.

We decree, any attempt at unauthorized voting will be revealed before it can take place. We declare those who vote and votes counted come only from American citizens who are registered to vote, with proper legal identification, living and true citizens. We declare any attempt to change the outcome of an election via unauthorized ballots and/or votes will not succeed in any city or state.

We declare voters will use wisdom as they cast their vote so that it not be wasted or stolen. Lord, give voters discerning hearts to vote for candidates who will do good for our nation and who will align with Your plans and purposes.

We declare any effort to illegally change the outcome of the election be exposed and stopped and that no weapon formed against our elections will prosper. Where there has been tampering in the past, we declare no more! We declare no stealthy manipulation, interference or hinderance will succeed to subvert or delay our elections or their outcome. We pray for Americans, who have given up on the election process due to corruption or dislike of candidates, to re-engage. We command apathy to go and be replaced with a desire to vote for righteous candidates to replace those who are compromised and corrupt.

We declare a fair and timely outcome in our elections. We pray that our elections will not be able to be shut down again or the in-person voting process stopped. Where they have weaponized mail-in ballots and tampered with voting machines, we pray that those avenues of corruption or internet interference will no longer be open to their manipulations. We declare those doors closed.

For those who have not taken the time to vote in years, we pray they will be convicted to vote again. May they take the time to research and pray for Your plan, purpose and candidate in each area for this nation to succeed.

You said those who deal truthfully are Your delight. So we ask that You place workers at each polling location who walk in truth and integrity. We declare and decree, in the mighty name of Jesus, there will be no ballot or machine rigging or illegal ballot harvesting. Any attempt at corruption will be immediately exposed and prosecuted to the fullest extent of the law. Shine Your light on our elections, and expose darkness and corruption so that the light of God will prevail.

We plead the blood of Jesus over all mail-in ballots. We assign angels to watch over all received and declare no illegal or duplicate votes will be counted. We declare protection in our elections so that boxes of ballots, which in the past have mysteriously appeared, will not be allowed and that legitimate ballots will not be lost or destroyed.

We declare that search engines and social media will have no influence or ability to censor or change the outcome of our elections. Where millionaires and billionaires have used their wealth to sway our elections, we pray that any such attempt, that may have worked in the past, will fall flat and will not prosper. We also pray any illegal actions or "donations" they have made to change the outcome of our elections will receive the just penalty due under the law.

We pray that voters will vote with wisdom for righteous candidates who stand for and with our Constitution. Forgive us where we have voted based on popularity, skin color, gender, or out of loyalty to a Party rather than loyalty to You.

Give us wisdom to see and hear beyond the political rhetoric to pay attention to actions, how candidates vote and how they live, which tells the true story.

Forgive us for being disengaged or unlearned about the political process and as a result have allowed it to be taken over.

We pray for any way in which corruption has wiggled its way into our election and voting process whether through voting machines, E-poll books, absentee ballots, voter rolls that haven't been updated, votes by dead people, ballot harvesting, etc. and we close each and every door in the spirit to theft and help us to close it in the natural.

As the election nears, help us remember our battle is not against flesh and blood but against rulers, principalities, and powers of darkness. Empower us to walk in this truth and not allow the Enemy to cause us to see people as the enemy. We ask for a spirit of repentance to sweep across our nation, that we return to a nation with a heart after You. Father, we pray for a holy fear of God to sweep across our land, leading us back to a place of rest on every side.

We pray for every person who calls on Your Name, that they will not waste their privilege to vote. If they are not registered, Holy Spirit compel them to do so now. If they have given up on the voting process, we pray that You would restore their hope and heart to be involved once again.

Help us to remember we aren't voting because we like or don't like a candidate, but because we love this nation and must stand fast for the freedoms afforded us in our Constitution. Forgive us where we have been complacent and allowed evil actors into leadership positions.

We pray that any and all attempts to manipulate or steal our votes, especially from the elderly, will be stopped. We pray for protection for those in nursing homes and in caregiver situations that their freedom to vote will not be taken from them or abused.

We pray for those, who have accepted the responsibility as delegates in each state, to be faithful to vote as they have been elected to do. We declare any corruption at the Republican National Convention or Democrat National Convention to be cast out and we close the door in prayer to evil actions, plans and deeds, and say they will not succeed.

Lord we thank you for the wisdom of our founding fathers in establishing the Electoral College. We pray it will not be destroyed or done away with, but that it would remain in place so that all Americans are represented in our election process. Where it has been denigrated, we pray that the truth of its importance will ring throughout our land and the lies over it will be dismantled. We declare the electoral votes for our state (and every state) would be counted fairly and never again would there be a certification of corrupt results. May the candidates elected be men and women who will humble themselves before You.

Father, we declare America will remain one nation under God and declare that as we humble ourselves before You, Your blessing would once again be upon this nation, our government and our election process.

Ex. 23:1-3, Dt. 3:22, Gal. 5:1, Is. 28:17, Pro. 14:34, Ps. 147:14, Job 22:28, Psalm 33:12, Jer. 9:3, James 1:5, 2 Cor. 10:4, 2 Chron. 7:14, 1 Kings 5:4

Prayer Over Elected Officials

You elected government officials to make decisions and it's about time they started making good ones.

*—Bob Riley
(52nd Governor of Alabama)*

We pray for President _____, and Vice-President _____ as well as our governors, congressmen, and mayors along with all those in authority over us that they would serve with the fear and reverence of the Lord. We pray they will be filled with Your wisdom and insight. That the eyes of their understanding would be opened to see and know the truth and that they would desire to operate in the truth. We pray that their minds would be renewed to the Word of God and that their hearts and minds would line up with Your plans and purposes for our nation. We pray that they will be people of integrity and honesty and that the American people can trust them. We declare they will have hearts like a stream of water that is turned toward You

We declare our elected officials will not take bribes, and corruption will be far from them. If they refuse to operate with integrity, we ask that You would expose it and that they would be removed from office. We pray that our nation would once again be respected as a country with strong and honorable leadership. Where there have been nefarious actions and those who have secretly established themselves as a shadow government intent on destroying America's freedom, we pray that warring angels would act on our behalf to confuse their communications and block their attempts to destabilize our nation, our economy and our safety.

If they have operated beyond the scope of their office or given our sovereignty to others, we declare any decision, alliance, or pact toward that end null and void. We pray You would restore what they have tried to steal or give to others.

We pray also for all elected officials in our cities, counties, and states including our sheriffs, school board members, city councilors, congressmen, justices, etc. Lord, we pray for godly men and women in those positions who will work for righteousness and Your agenda for America and not their own. We ask that You would open their eyes to see and know the truth and to come into the knowledge of You. For those that refuse, we pray they would be removed and replaced by men and women who will honor You and our Constitution.

For all of these leaders we ask that You remove all selfish ambition from their hearts, and that it would be replaced with a hunger to walk in the wisdom that comes from You which is pure, peace-loving, gentle, full of mercy and good fruit, impartial and sincere.

May they display high moral integrity and character in every decision they make. Remind them of why they ran for office. Remind them of their commitment to build a better, safer dwelling place over the area in which they serve.

We come against the spirit of division in our land and we say NO MORE! You are loosed from your assignment and we bind to our nation a spirit of unity and love. Where seeds of discord and riots have been sown, we uproot them now in prayer and we speak unity into the racial divide, gender divide, minority divide, political divide and Christian divide. We uproot confusion, strife and every evil work and we loose a spirit of peace, harmony and revival into our land. We say COME FORTH! We declare that America will love You with all their heart, soul, mind strength, and our neighbor as ourselves. Lord bring true reconciliation that only You can provide as hearts are changed to acknowledge You first.

We ask You to turn the ear of our governor, congressmen and mayors to You each day that they will apply Your wisdom to every decision they make.

We ask if there are any who do not know You, that they would turn their heart to You and serve You in their personal life as well as their political life.

If there are any that will not bow their knee to You, remove them God and put men and women who walk in righteousness in their place. Cause them to vote and take action that honors what is in the best interest of the people of their state.

We ask for leaders who will humble themselves and pray. We ask for spiritually mature leaders who will worship You and praise You, in spirit and in truth. That our elected officials will seek You for wisdom, insight and direction and will obey Your voice. We pray that they will have ears to hear and will hear Your voice above the noise and chaos. We pray any unholy alliances will be severed and if they are trusting any they should not, reveal it to them now.

When they speak may their words be truthful. Holy Spirit we ask that You would fill their mouth with Your words.

God we ask that both our elected and non-elected officials would not overreach with their authority. Let them not abuse their power. We decree, they will daily uphold our freedom and our constitutional rights. Thank You Lord for hearing our prayer for our leaders in Your mighty Name we pray.

Psalm 2:10-11, Prov 21:1, Col 1:9, Eph 1:18, Prov 2:1-8, Jn 8:32, Eph 4:23, James 3:15-17, Mark 12:30-31

Coup Creators & Stolen Seats

For the entire four years of the greatest presidential term of our lifetime, Democrats led by Speaker Pelosi and radical socialists in her party attempted coup after coup against President Donald Trump.[19]

—Marjorie Taylor Greene

Father, we continue to keep our eyes on You as the one true God. We know that You are in control and nothing is too difficult for You. You see the deceitful plans they have concocted to achieve a global one-world government and control. They have conceived trouble and given birth to evil as their wombs fashion deceit. Save us Lord from lying lips and from deceitful tongues who create falsehoods to propel their plans.

We pray not only for the restoration of our nation but for those who masterminded the coup attempt and all who followed along with it. We pray that their hearts of stone would be turned to hearts of flesh to repent before it is too late.

Send laborers across their paths to speak truth and may they repent of the evil, the lies and the deceit that they have unleashed on our nation. May they fear God and get a glimpse of the eternity that lies before them if they do not repent. We know You take no pleasure in the death of the wicked. And so we pray that the wicked will turn from their wicked ways and live. We say "Turn back, turn back from your evil ways, for why will you die in your wickedness because there is a day coming…"

We will not give up in our fight for truth, freedom and Your Kingdom. We plant our feet firmly on Your Word which does not return void. We pray that all factual evidence, that has been dispelled, hidden or overlooked, would no longer be able to be dismissed. May this fight for truth continue until the truth of what transpired no longer be ignored. Expose all bribery, extortion, kickbacks, and every other wicked financial dealing in government. We ask that the evidence against their takeover and election interference stand up in court.

We pray for wise and skillful prosecutors to rise up who will prosecute these cases and win. That trickery, unrighteous judges and loopholes they have used would no longer be available to allow them an escape for their crimes. May every thief and perpetrator be brought to justice and convicted where guilty, but we also pray You would show mercy to all who will receive it.

Father, You see their agenda to implement a mandatory digital currency, ESG, facial recognition software, vaccine passports and more. Deliver us and rescue us Lord for we cry out to You.

Like Jehoshaphat, in days of old we pray, "Our God, will you not judge them? For we have no power to face this vast army that is attacking us. We do not know what to do, but our eyes are on you."

We declare Your Word that You will rescue us from every evil attack and will bring us safely to Your heavenly kingdom. We will tread on the lion and the cobra. We will trample the great lion and the serpent. Because we love You, You said You would rescue us and protect us, because we acknowledge Your name. As we call on

You answer us, be with us in trouble to deliver us and honor us. For we know You will not forsake us or leave us.

We declare Your plans and purposes will prevail! We declare revival is coming and will transform hearts as they cry out to You for help. We declare America will be saved. We declare revival is spreading like wildfire and cannot be stopped for Your glory will be revealed and Your name exalted.

Father God, we call on You as the righteous judge that these crimes will be prosecuted and no longer swept under the rug or ignored. We ask You to expose what needs to be exposed; rout criminals and criminal dealings out of government; and replace them with righteous leaders who love You, who will steward our resources well, and will fight for righteousness, truth and justice.

Give us righteous leaders who will preserve America and our Constitution for the sake of our children, and our children's children.

Jer 32:17, Job 15:35, Ps 120:2, Ez 36:26, Ez 33:11, Prov 6:30-31, 2 Chron 20:12, 2 Tim 4:18, Ps 90:13-15, I Peter 5:9

Regarding the National Debt

Father, we have become a debtor nation and we repent. It has enslaved us to other nations. We pray that our governmental leaders, at every level, would be wise stewards. We declare a stop to the ungodly legislation that has continued to be passed which adds to our debt as it enriches our enemies and steals from our children.

We repent of our lack of godly stewardship and ask that You would convict the hearts of those who have used their position to pad their own pockets and increase our debt to increase their favor, position, power and wealth.

May we have a holy fear of mishandling the resources You have entrusted to us and blessed us with. Help us to wisely steward what You have given us and show us how to get out of this enormous debt that is choking our nation.

As Abraham followed and obeyed You, You blessed him even in a land where he was a foreigner and under famine. We know what You did then You can do now. We ask for a turnaround of this precarious position they created to impoverish us and our children.

We declare that their fiscal irresponsibility will be upon their own heads and their wicked plans exposed. Where they gave millions and billions of our taxpayer dollars to other countries for wicked schemes, we pray for restoration. We declare the wealth of the wicked has been stored up for the righteous and as we toss our "bread" upon the water and have helped many nations in crisis, that it is coming back to us on every wave.

We pray as it is returned that we would steward it well and use it for Your purposes.

Prov 22:7, Gen 28:4, Prov 13:22, Ecc 11

FOR RIGHTEOUS JUDGES

"The due administration of justice is the firmest pillar of good government, I have considered the first arrangement of the judicial department as essential to the happiness of the country, and to the stability of its political system."[20]

—George Washington

We pray for the U.S. Attorney General and the attorney general in each state across our land. We pray that they will be forthright men/women of integrity as their positions demand. We declare they are free from corruption and so are able, without hesitation, to investigate corruption. If corrupt and wicked individuals are holding those positions, any who take bribes or succumb to blackmail, we declare their day of corruption over and that they would no longer be able to remain in those positions, but be replaced with those who will fear God and not man.

We pray for the judges and justices in our land from the U.S. Supreme Court and to every court in America. We have grown weary of an expectation for justice that has not been fulfilled. For there are many who hold these positions who do not judge as in days of old when You raised up judges who delivered Your people from the hands of those who plundered them.

May the fear of God come upon all who hold these positions for that is the beginning of wisdom. For even the unjust judge gave the widow woman justice, how much more will You give justice to Your children. You will see to it that justice is done for Your people who cry out to You day and night and we pray that it is done soon.

For rulers, leaders and judges should hold no terror for those who do right, but for those who do wrong. And yet, that is not what we are experiencing. Lord we pray that those who have abused their positions, and have trampled on justice, to experience justice and be prosecuted and replaced with the justice they have ignored.

We pray into our courts godly judges, whether appointed or elected, to be chosen because they possess godly wisdom, act with integrity, are fair and just, and honor our Constitution.

You said, a false witness will not go unpunished, and whoever pours out lies will not go free. We declare that those who have poured out lies, who have ignored our laws, who have rewritten them to support their evil plans, will be exposed and brought to justice and that the truth will be brought into the light.

Prov 19:5, Judges 2:16, Prov 9:10, Luke 18:7-8, Romans 13:3-4, Prov 19:5

The Media

Before mass leaders seize the power to fit reality to their lies, their propaganda is marked by its extreme contempt for facts as such, for in their opinion fact depends entirely on the power of man who can fabricate it.[21]

—Hannah Arendt

We declare over every media source: radio, television, print, online, social media, etc., that they return to truth or that their doors will be shut and their ability to deceive will come to an end. Where our media has become little more than a propaganda mouthpiece in the attempt to destroy our Republic, we declare that their lying lips will be silenced. Let the wicked be put to shame; let them lie silent in Sheol. Silence the lips that speak with arrogance against the righteous, full of pride and contempt. For we know Your goodness is great which You have laid up for those who fear You, which You have bestowed on those who take refuge in You!

Hide Donald Trump, America, and Your people in the secret place of Your Presence from the schemes of evil men and women who use our media to spread division, lies and violence. Conceal us in Your shelter from accusing tongues and false accusations.

We declare that like Balaam in the days of old, the media who desire to speak or write a curse or lie, will be unable to do so. That despite their effort to spread falsehood, they will be compelled to share the truth. We declare that no longer will the lying media reports go unchallenged, but each media outlet that continues printing and speaking lies rather than truth will be like Ananias and Sapphira[22], struck down, or bankrupted and their doors closed. May the demise of those organizations be swift so that all will know that our God is in control.

We pray for a resurgence of media who will speak, write and publish truth. For journalists who will investigate both sides of a story with honesty and integrity and who are unwilling to be manipulated by prejudice or threat.

Hear our cry O Lord and attend unto our prayer, for we cry out to You regarding the lies that have been poured out over America like water. They have been poured into our young people, against our nation and Truth and have brought fear and confusion. We ask for Your intervention so that the Truth would be revealed and restored.

We declare all lies exposed. Bring them down to the ground and let truth once again reign in its place. Father, You said lying lips are an abomination to You, but those who act faithfully are Your delight. Take delight in us as we call out those who speak with lying lips for You said You would judge between the righteous and the unrighteous. We call upon You to do that and show yourself strong in our nation.

We bind the lying spirits that have been unleashed. For you said what is bound in heaven, is bound on earth. You said a false witness will not go unpunished, and whoever pours out lies will perish. Lord may the fear of God come upon our land so that those who speak lies are quickly exposed and dealt with and all will see it is You that have brought it about.

The Media

Where they have silenced and censored truth seeking to confuse and deceive, we bind the spirit of deception and lies controlling the media and we declare its assignment finished. We take authority over the lying spirits and declare they can speak out their lies no more.

Lord just as you shut the lion's mouths in the days of Daniel, so they could not devour and consume him, so we ask that you would shut the mouths of the media who seek to destroy and consume our nation.

We ask that You would not be silent regarding this issue. For the wicked and the deceitful have opened their mouths against us, against Donald Trump and against America —which You love. They have spoken hateful words with a forked tongue. They have surrounded us and fought against us without cause. We declare for those who walk in integrity that they will walk securely, but those who take crooked paths will be found out.

O Lord, deliver us from their hand and may those who refuse to bow their knee to the name of Jesus, if they refuse to speak truth, may they be removed and their places given to those who will walk in humility and truth.

Ps 31:17-20, Ps 61:1, Prov 12:22, Prov 19:9,
Prov 10:9, Ps 109:8, Is. 37:20

Freedom of Speech

"Whoever would overthrow the liberty of a nation must begin by subduing the freeness of speech."[23]

—*Benjamin Franklin*

We thank You Lord that we have had the opportunity to live in America with great liberty and freedom that many countries do not possess. Forgive us where we took it for granted. We pray now regarding America's Bill of Rights which is under threat. We pray it will not be destroyed or further chipped away, but restored by Your mighty hand. We pray especially in regards to our freedom of speech which has been under severe attack.

We declare that freedom of speech will be restored. Where it has been silenced, including on school campuses, where conservative speakers and students have been silenced and/or removed; in our media, where freedom of speech was once honored, but which has now been made a mockery; in our courts and every other place where the freedom of speech has been trampled, we declare restoration now.

We pray for discernment for the American people and all over the globe. We bind the spirit of deception that has clouded minds and eyes and declare the eyes of their understanding be enlightened so that they can recognize the truth from a lie.

Where the spirit of the Lord is there is liberty, so we declare the spirit of the Lord to be poured out upon every place and venue where truth and freedom of speech has been silenced. But even as we pray for freedom of speech to be restored as well as for other freedoms previously afforded us which have been stolen, we pray we would not use our freedom to indulge the flesh, but rather, serve one another humbly in love.

Where arrogant and evil men and women, some who sit as judges in our land, have unjustly used their authority and power to prevent and block facts and truth, who deny us freedom of speech, we pray that the prison door put in place to prevent our freedom of speech, be unlocked and opened so that truth can once again flow.

Eph 1:18, Matt 18:18, 2 Cor 3:17, Gal 5:13

Exposure of Corruption

"There may be times when we are powerless to prevent injustice, but there must never be a time when we fail to protest."

—*Elie Wiesel*
Nobel laureate, and Holocaust survivor

We declare that we will not remain silent in the face of corruption and injustice. We take this time to declare the Word of God to bind and renounce corruption and injustice that has been allowed to grow in our nation and push back against the darkness and deceit. We declare that it will not continue but that it must bow to righteousness and truth.

We declare:

- Woe to those who declare the wicked innocent for a bribe, and take away the rights of the ones who are in the right!

- Woe to the wicked! It shall be ill with them: for the reward of their hands shall be given them.

- Woe to those who enact unjust laws and to those who constantly record harmful decisions, so as to deprive the needy of justice and rob the poor among Your people of their rights, so that widows may be their spoil and that they may plunder the orphans. Now what will we do in the day of punishment, and in the devastation which will come from afar? To whom will we flee for help? And where will we leave our wealth?

- We flee to You Lord, the maker of heaven and earth to right these wrongs and deliver us from evil!

- Woe to those who go to great depths to hide their plans from the Lord, who do their work in darkness and think, "Who sees us? Who will know?"

- YOU know Lord and nothing escapes Your sight. Deliver us from their wicked schemes.

- We declare justice will be done, and criminal actions, many which have already been exposed, now be prosecuted before fair and honest judges. May the perpetuators finally be held accountable for their criminal actions. We declare that Americans will have the courage to look at the truth as it is revealed and that as justice is restored it will bring joy to the righteous and terror to evildoers.

Is 5:23, Is 10:1-3, Is 3:11, Is 29:15, Prov 21:15

Truth Regarding 2020 Election & Protection Over Upcoming Elections

"Injustice anywhere is a threat to justice everywhere.[24]

—Martin Luther King, Jr.

Father, we come to You today concerning the 2020 presidential election and the mountain of evidence of irregularities and illegalities that have been ignored. Much has been brought into the light and yet still we have not seen justice regarding the outcome of that election and what took place. We plead the blood of Jesus over the search for righteous judges who will have the courage to not just look at the evidence but side with justice and truth. Give them courage and protect them and their families as they take a stand against evil. We pray for the Holy Spirit to come upon the judges in our land that they will fear God rather than man and will be compelled to do the right thing and do their jobs with integrity.

We declare that all who planned and participated in the collaborative effort to stop the investigation into the irregularities of the 2020 election, by creating the "insurrection" of January 6 so that the certification of the votes would continue, will be held accountable for what they did. As they have continued their attempts to charge Donald Trump with treason from what took place that day, may their own words and determination to indict him and imprison him come back on them for the treasonous actions *they* committed. May there be a reversal anywhere that allowed people to be seated in offices, who were not elected fairly by the people.

We declare that the coup attempt this nation has suffered, which has resulted in the destruction of our economy, our borders, our trust in government and where they are working to give away our sovereignty, will come to an end and each person who planned it or aligned with it brought to justice. We pray for a reversal of all they have done to destroy America, our freedoms and remove You and duly elected leaders from our land.

We thank You for the states that have either decertified the vote from that election or are in the process. May those investigations continue and may state governmental leaders have the courage to act on the evidence that has come to light.

We thank You for all who have spent the last several years of their own time and resources traveling the nation to expose the corruption and show the irrefutable evidence of theft and illegalities. We pray for blessing and restoration of their time, money and businesses for the sacrifices they have made to make sure that this could not be swept under the rug and forever hidden.

Where people have been unwilling to acknowledge the truth or have been blinded by a spirit of pride, offense and deception, we command those blinders to be removed so that no longer can people say it didn't happen when it did. Open their eyes Lord.

Where the media, the evil perpetrators of deception, have continued to spew out their lies as fact, we declare that their lies will fall to the ground and will not go unpunished for You detest lying lips. We declare over every person who joined hands in agreement with this plan that none would escape the spotlight of revelation and justice that is coming.

You saw the leaders who participated in Joe Biden's inaugural ceremony as they nervously looked around in the bizarre two-minute silence during the swearing-in ceremony. We declare that their determination to keep their actions hidden, and their attempt to do it again, will be thwarted. Confuse their communication and plans as you did at the Tower of Babel. For You hate hearts that devise wicked plans and false witnesses who speak lies. We declare no weapon formed against this nation and our upcoming elections will prosper.

We declare and decree, that all unauthorized voting that took place, by people without legal identification, those who voted multiple times, who were not citizens, who stuffed mailboxes with ballots, who stole and submitted votes for people in nursing homes, who rigged machines, who concealed the truth, that ALL illegal and unauthorized votes, even at this late date, will be revealed and thrown out. Expose, expose, expose what was done in the darkness so that not only it is brought fully into the light, but prosecuted to the fullest extent of the law.

We declare, as a result, we will return to paper ballots and elections in which the multiple avenues of theft are no longer possible.

We declare their ongoing attempt to charge Donald Trump with treason to subvert his ability to become president again will not succeed and that the truth regarding what took place during the 2020 election will finally not only be brought fully into the light, but fully accepted.

Proverbs 6:16-19, Proverbs 12:22, Proverbs 19:9, Gen 11:7, Proverbs 19:21, Is 54:17, Eph 5:13

RELEASE OF POLITICAL PRISONERS

"Where justice is denied, where poverty is enforced, where ignorance prevails, and where any one class is made to feel that society is an organized conspiracy to oppress, rob and degrade them, neither persons nor property will be safe."[25]

—Frederick Douglass

Father, we come before You on behalf of the political prisoners arrested on January 6, 2021. Some are still held unjustly in prison, denied justice, in conditions that we have not even allowed for murderers and terrorists. We pray for a speedy and divine intervention for their release and restoration to their families of what was stolen from them. We pray that they will not grow weary in their stand for righteousness and truth. Where their rights have been trampled, we pray for restitution and release.

Some have admitted guilt to things they didn't so they could be released. Where that has happened, we pray that their reputations and record be cleared.

We know some acted in violence that day. We pray that all judgments given are fair and equitable to crimes committed. We also know from video evidence and testimony that Capitol police invited people into the building, who were later charged with trespassing. We know that some of those officers were also instigators setting off flash bombs to create confusion and fear. We now know some in the FBI, dressed as Trump supporters, were used to instigate violence and create chaos. We know much of what was shown to the American public was staged for television to look like one thing on live television, when those who actually saw and recorded events, know it was very different from what was portrayed. We pray that those who created this narrative, who planned this insurgence, who tried to set this up against Donald Trump, will be exposed and prosecuted fully.

Former Speaker of the House Nancy Pelosi and Washington, D.C. Mayor Muriel Bowser did everything in their power to create an environment ripe for chaos and punish any who attended the peaceful event where patriots gathered to protest the irregularities of the 2020 election. Their actions were preplanned and intentional and yet they seemed to have escaped justice. Your Word says You will bring disaster on them which they will not be able to escape. And because of their unrepentant hearts, though they cry to You, You will not listen to them.

Where patriots were indicted because they refused to bow to the schemes and attempts to gather information against President Trump, we pray that the evil indictments against them would be reversed and removed. The wicked laughed at their ability to arrest patriots and silence Donald Trump over the events of that day. They made promises that they would go after those who were either part of his administration or dared to testify on his behalf. May their threats fall to the ground. You said evil men/women are held captive by their own sins and which are as ropes that catch and hold them. May it be so.

Your Word says that all rulers You have established hold no terror for those who do right, but for those who do wrong. That if we want to be free from fear of the one in authority then all we need to do is what is right and we will be commended. This administration is not that and therefore proves they are not established by You according to the criteria of Your Word.

Evidence clearly shows we did not vote them in and now the righteous have reason to fear their retribution. Lord, we ask that You not hold us accountable for their corrupt actions and ungodly ways. May the trap they have laid, they fall into themselves. Keep the righteous and those unjustly charged with a crime, safe from the traps set by these evildoers, from the snares they have laid for them. Be a strong tower they can run into for safety against this evil.

Father, we stand in the gap and pray on behalf of all political prisoners and those around the world persecuted for righteousness' sake. It is wicked. You see how the wicked seem to prosper and mock as they threaten and persecute those who have stood against unrighteousness. Sweep away the violence of the wicked, those who refuse to do justice.

Lord, we do not pray for their destruction, but for them to repent and know You. But if they refuse, may they be removed and their influence and ability to manipulate be destroyed. May their grip of evil over our nation and around the world be broken. Your Word says, "In a little while, the wicked will be no more; though we look for them, they will not be found." So be it.

Gal 6:9, Jer 11:11, Prov 5:22, Romans 13:3, Prov 26:27, Ps 141:9, Prov 18:10, Prov 21:7, Ps 37:10

PRAYERS FOR AMERICA TO WAKE UP!

"Throughout history, it has been the inaction of those who could have acted; the indifference of those who should have known better; the silence of the voice of justice when it mattered most; that has made it possible for evil to triumph."[26]

—*Haile Selassie*
(Emperor of Ethiopia - 1930 to 1974)

Father, we rejoice in You and celebrate You as the Creator of the world and our Maker.

You made heaven, the heaven of heavens, with all their host, the earth and all that is on it, the seas and all that is in them; and You preserve all of them. The host of heaven worships You and we pray for revival in America that we will join them!

We recognize what You have done in the past to deliver Your people and ask that You do it again. May the words of our mouth and the meditation of our heart be acceptable in Your sight Lord, our strength and our redeemer. We forgive and release all who have hurt or betrayed us and release all disappointment of any kind that would allow offense and keep us blinded to the truth.

We repent on behalf of our nation and the pride, perversion, corruption and apathy that has brought us to this place. We thank you for this opportunity to repent for ourselves, on behalf of our families, our government, and our nation.

We declare that we will see the goodness of God in the land of the living.

We humble ourselves before You as we recognize that pride opens the door to deception. We ask You to reveal any area of pride in our lives so that we can uproot it. And we pray it off of our nation. Let not the foot of pride come upon us, our families, our church, our nation. We command it to bow its knee and that any darkness or mist that has covered our eyes, any area of deception it has allowed that has blinded our eyes, to be removed. We say go now!

We also pray over our leaders, pastors, the media, our nation, and our families that You would give us a spirit of wisdom and revelation in the knowledge of You. I pray that the eyes of our heart would be enlightened so that we will know what is the hope of Your calling in our lives and nation. That we would know the riches of the glory of Your inheritance to the saints, and the surpassing greatness of Your power toward us who believe in accordance with the working of the strength of Your might. We declare WAKE UP to America and the world. May we see Your might and the undeniable demonstration of Your power which brings people to repentance.

We bind the spirit of witchcraft and deception in our land and release the Spirit of Truth to prevail. Where eyes have been blinded to truth, we say, "Wake up!" and declare that veil removed so we can return to truth. Help us to see as You see. Give us wisdom, insight and understanding to see from Your perspective for You said we are seated with You in heavenly places.

We declare that the spirit of apathy be cast out and cast into the sea. Where our nation has been under the spell of witchcraft, we bind it and cast it off and pray that it will be replaced with a spirit of truth and that people will hunger again for the Word of Truth and Word of God. Awaken our hearts and open our eyes to the desperate need of this hour to fast and pray for Your glory to be revealed. May we not be willing to stay holed up in our homes in fear, but instead press into You to pray for reformation and revival and heart transformation.

We declare that we are renewed in the spirit of our mind which after God is created in righteousness and true holiness. And that those who have been caught in the web of deception would come to their senses and escape from the snare of the devil that has held them captive to do his will.

We pray that those who err in their mind will know the truth and those who criticize will accept instruction. That as pride bows its knee to You Lord, so also must be the spirit of hate, criticism and shaming that has been unleashed. We uproot it now in prayer. We declare that Your transforming love and revival will fill our land, our homes, our churches, our businesses and our government. Where division and hate have ruled, we declare that hearts are being transformed by the power of God, so that the hearts of the fathers will be turned to the children and the hearts of the children to the fathers. We declare the knowledge of the glory of the Lord will cover the earth—including America—as the waters cover the sea.

Neh 9:6, Ps 19:14, Ps 27:13, Ps. 36:11, Eph 1:17-19, Eph 4:23, Eph 2:6, 2 Tim 2:26, Isaiah 29:24, Mal 4:6, Hab 2:14

COURAGE FOR AMERICANS TO STAND

"You just need to be a flea against injustice. Enough committed fleas biting strategically can make even the biggest dog uncomfortable and transform even the biggest nation."

—*attributed to Marian Wright Edelman*

Forgive us Lord where we have exchanged courage and liberty for the promise of safety. When others stood against injustice, rather than stand with them, due to fear we closed our eyes and let them face persecution alone. Forgive us.

We do not want to be named among the cowardly, unbelieving, abominable, murderers, sexually immoral, sorcerers, idolaters, or liars, for they will be cast into the lake of fire and brimstone —the second death. We repent of cowardice— and any other sin named. Strengthen us to have courage mixed with wisdom. To know when to speak and act even as we pray.

Let us be named among those who overcome, that we and our families will inherit Your promises.

Lord, We ask, that like the disciples in Acts, when threatened to stop speaking about You, they prayed for more courage so they could speak more. Their prayer is ours! So now, Lord, look at their threats, and grant to us, Your servants, to speak Your Word with all confidence. Lord, extend Your hand to heal. We pray for revival and we ask for signs and wonders to take place through the name of Your holy servant Jesus.

Bring revival Lord that will cause every knee to bow and every tongue to confess You as Lord!

Lord, we command the spirit of fear and cowardice, that has tried to intimidate and silence Your Church and people, to go. We pray for an infusion of Your strength and courage. You said You have not given us a spirit of fear, but of power, love and a sound mind. We declare it is ours and may the feelings follow.

We pray over our leaders, judges, pastors, and families that where there has been cowardice you will infuse courage. You said that You shelter us under Your wings. Lord for those who fear reprisal or attack, show them You are well able to protect.

We know You look down from heaven. You see all humankind. From where You sit enthroned, You watch all the inhabitants of the earth. You who fashions the hearts of us all, and observes all our deeds, said that a king is not saved by his great army; a warrior is not delivered by his great strength. The war horse is a vain hope for victory, and by its great might it cannot save. Let our trust not be in those things, or in our own power, but in You. Truly Your eye is on those who fear You, on those who hope in Your steadfast love, to deliver our souls from death, and to keep us alive, even in famine.

Our soul waits for You O Lord for You are our help and shield. Our heart is glad in You, because we trust in Your holy name. Let Your steadfast love, O Lord, be upon us, even as we hope in You.

Rev 21:7-8, Acts 4:29-30, Rom 14:11, 2 Tim 1:7, Ps 91:4, Ps 33:12-22

Protection From Violence and Intimidation

"There is a stubbornness about me that never can bear to be frightened at the will of others. My courage always rises at every attempt to intimidate me."[27]

—Jane Austen, Pride and Prejudice

Father, Your Word tells us when we come into agreement, we will have what we have asked of you. Today, we come into agreement for the protection and safety of our families and our nation. We bind the spirit of violence and intimidation and tell it to leave our lives and leave our nation, this day in Jesus's name.

The works of the flesh are evident, including outbursts of wrath, selfish ambitions, dissensions, heresies, envy, murders, drunkenness, and revelries…yet Your Word says You will rescue us from all evildoers and protect us from the violent. Your unchanging Word says You will keep us and our nation safe from those who have evil plans in their heart, and those who stir up war. We remind You of Your promise today as we declare…

No weapon formed against us or our nation will prosper. We declare it is only with our eyes that we will see the reward of the wicked. A thousand may fall by our side, but it will not come near us.

We declare and decree You are protecting us from all violence for we are precious in Your sight. We declare this day, You have not given us a spirit of fear but of power, love and a sound mind and we walk in peace all the days of our life.

We will not fear our adversaries, for our protection is from You. We refuse to be afraid of their threats and we will not be troubled in Jesus's name. We stand firm and bold in our faith and peace.

Father, we declare, according to Your Word that violence shall no longer be heard in our land, neither wasting nor destruction in our borders, but our walls shall be called salvation and our gates praise.

Your Word says, that You will punish those who fill our houses with violence and deceit. We ask You to look upon our nation and remove from our land those who desire to promote violence and destruction. Remove those who are sowing fear and deception and who refuse to bow their knee to You.

According to Your Word, this day we ask You to remove their violence, plundering, and intimidation and execute justice and righteousness in our nation this day.

Matt 18:19-21, Is 54:17, Ps 72:14, 2 Tim 1:7, Phil 1:28, 1 Peter 3:14, Is 60:18, Deut 31:6, Zeph 1:9, Ez 45:9, Matt 28:20

AMERICA TO BE RESTORED

The last day of the Constitutional Convention of September 18, 1787 a lady asked Dr. Benjamin Franklin, "Well Doctor, what have we got a republic or a monarchy?" "A republic — if you can keep it."[28]

—Benjamin Franklin

Father, today we come before you on behalf of our nation. We repent of our wicked ways. We humble ourselves before You and ask You to forgive our sins and heal our land.

We seek the peace and prosperity of our city and nation. Today, we pray to You for the welfare of our city and our nation, knowing their welfare will determine ours.

We stand in our spiritual authority over our nation and declare it is our possession. It is the place You have given us to dwell in and to exercise our authority. We declare our nation will again drink water from the rain of heaven. It is a land which You care for and Your eyes are always on our nation, from the beginning of the year to the very end.

We thank You that Your thoughts for our nation are thoughts of peace and not evil, to give us a good future and continuous hope.

We bow our hearts before You this day and we repent of the sins of America. We ask You to forgive us and cleanse our land from all unrighteousness. We ask for a divine visitation of the Holy Spirit in America and declare revival is coming. May our nation, as a whole, turn back to You. We plead the blood of Jesus over this land and declare You are Lord over America as was established at its birth.

We take authority over every negative word that has been spoken over our nation and every evil plan spoken against it. We uproot them now in prayer and declare them null and void. We pull down every curse and pronouncement of witchcraft against our nation, our churches and our leaders and declare those curses powerless and unable to produce fruit.

We declare fear cannot reside in our nation and must go in Jesus's name. We declare God rules and reigns over America again and from this day forward. We bind the spirit of division that has been unleashed and cast it out of our homes and nation. We declare in its place that unity reigns and where there is unity, God commands the blessing of life evermore.

Therefore we declare that America is filled with the life and glory of God.

2 Chron 7:14, Jer 29:7, Deut 11:10-12, Jer 29:11, Neh 1:6-7, 1 Jn 1:9, Ps 133:3

Our Prophetic Declaration Over America

What are prophetic declarations? They are when we take the Word of God and declare it over a situation. It is not foretelling, it is forthtelling.

No matter how bleak the situation, we are told the Word brings life. We are to call those things that are not as though they were. We are told to speak to the dry bones. We are told that the heroes of faith saw, spoke and operated from a different vantage point. And so should we. With that in mind, we make this prophetic declaration over America.

May we align our words with THE WORD and quit agreeing with the darkness.

- ★ We declare that the righteous will once again be in authority in America, so that the people will rejoice. We say that America WILL fulfill her destiny and return to her foundation as "one nation under God" (Prov 29:2).

- ★ We declare that America will not be aligned with a "throne of destruction" that refuses to align with You or honor You. We declare that those who devise mischief by decree and band themselves together against the life of the righteous, those who condemn the innocent to death, that this will NOT be America's future, and they will be removed. We pray instead that America will value and protect life, righteous decrees and Truth. That America will honor You and that

Your glory would cover the earth as the waters cover the sea (Ps 94:20-22, Hab 2:14).

★ We declare that righteous men and women will flourish and that they will not be removed or censored for standing up against unrighteousness (Ps 93:12).

★ We declare that as righteousness and justice are the foundation of Your throne, so they will be the foundation of America and our government once again. RESTORE righteousness and justice O Lord. We declare that godly men and women of integrity, who honor You and who will make righteous judgments and decisions, will be restored to places of authority (Ps 89:14).

★ We declare the angel of the Lord encamps around all who fear You and rescues us from evil men. Lord deliver us from unrighteousness and evil. We declare that America is blessed because we take refuge in You. We declare that unrighteous judges and leaders would be exposed and cast out of their places by Your mighty hand. (Ps 34:7-9)

★ We declare that You are our refuge and strength, a very present help in time of trouble, therefore we will not fear. May the spirit of fear that has been poured out upon our land be uprooted and no longer be a controlling force in our nation (Ps 46:1-2).

★ We declare that You will redeem, our soul and our nation in peace from the battle which is against us. For there are many who strive with us (Ps 55:18).

★ There are many who fight proudly against us, but we declare when we are afraid, we will put our trust in You — in God, whose Word we praise. What can mere man do to us? (Ps 56:2 & 4).

★ Woe to those who enact evil statutes and to those who constantly record unjust decisions to deprive the needy of justice. We declare the restoration of our leaders as in days of old and our rulers as at the beginning—for those who fear and reverence Your name (Is 10:1, Is 1:26).

★ We declare that the yoke of the burden of unjust taxes, "relief" bills that drain our nation, ungodly mandates and shutdowns to close places of worship will be broken from our neck and our shackles torn away" (Is 9: 4, Nah 1:13).

★ We declare that we will run and not be weary. We will walk and not faint. That you have sent Your Word to heal us and deliver us from our destructions (Is. 40: 31, Ps 107:20).

★ We will arise and shine and declare Your light has come and the glory of the Lord has risen upon America. For behold darkness will cover the earth, and deep darkness the peoples, but the Lord will again arise upon America and her people and His glory will appear upon us and nation will come to the Light. We declare REVIVAL, repentance and restoration in our nation to once again be a country that honors You (Is 60:1-3).

★ We declare that Your Name will be profaned no more. And the nations will know that You are the Lord. Behold it is coming and it shall be done (Ez 39:7-8).

★ We declare that the righteous man/woman will flourish and not be removed or censored. (Ps 93:12)

CAN AMERICA BE SAVED?

Only God can move mountains, but faith & prayer can move God.[29]
—E.M. Bounds

I hear some say we should no longer pray over America. I am always shocked and disheartened by that statement. I believe we are called to pray over our leaders and nation and that without the prayers of the Remnant, America cannot be saved.

I read the book of Revelation, and like many question where is America. I realize that there are references that perhaps could be about America, but to be clear, it isn't clear. Does that mean America is gone? Or perhaps no longer strong enough as a nation to be relevant?

We don't know. Even if we are assured of that answer, I see nowhere in the Bible the instruction to stop praying.

John Wesley once said, "God does nothing but by prayer, and everything with it." What I know is that if we don't pray, God will not act.

As the last names were being signed on the Declaration of Independence, Benjamin Franklin, made an observation about the chair that Washington had been sitting in as he presided over the Convention. The chair had an emblem of half of a sun. Franklin noted that artists often have a hard time distinguishing between a rising and a setting sun in their artwork. "I have often and often, in the course of the session, and the vicissitudes of my hopes and fears as to its issue, looked at that behind the President, without being able to tell whether it was rising or setting: but now at length, I have the happiness to know, that it is a rising and not a setting sun."[30]

And as we pray, may it continue to rise rather than allowing the sun to set on America.

Our prayers avail much.

If this book has been a blessing to you in some way. Or if you have additional questions, I would love to hear from you. You can reach me at:

Mail: PO Box 700515,
Tulsa, OK 74170 U.S.A.

E-mail: karen@lightandremnant.org

Or you can check out my websites and social media:

Website: prioritypr.org
Website: karenhardin.com
Website: City-by-City Prayer Network - city-by-city.org
Prophetic Insights: karenhardin.com/blog/

JOIN THE MOVEMENT!

Each Monday morning we send a prayer email targeting a specific issue in our nation for prayer.

Join the City-by-City Prayer Network and thousands across our nation and the globe as we pray for our nation. There is no fee to join.

The purpose of City-by-City intercessors is to take back our cities from corruption and perversity which is marching across our land. Our goal is to raise up at least ten people in every city across our nation and around the world who will stand and pray in their seat of authority—their city—to see revival.

Abraham interceded before the Lord for the sake of Sodom and Gomorrah.

"Will you sweep away the righteous with the wicked? What if there are fifty righteous people in the city? Will you really sweep it away and not spare the place for the sake of the fifty righteous people in it?

He continued to plead with the Lord until finally he said, "May the Lord not be angry, but let me speak just once more. What if only ten can be found there?"

He answered, "For the sake of ten, I will not destroy it."[69]

Each Monday morning check your inbox for the City-by-City scriptural prayer and governmental insights for that week. If you would like to join and stand for your city, go to: https://city-by-city.org/register/

Karen has several free scriptural prayers available for download which include:

- How to Overcome in Adverse Situations
- Healing Is Mine! Scriptural Prayers
- Stand Fast: How to Pray in Uncertain Times
- He Will Provide: Scriptural Prayer Decrees for Provision
- Secure the Borders of Your Home: Scriptural Prayer Decrees for You and your Family
- Prayer of Confession and Repentance and a Cry for Revival
- Prayer of Breakthrough for America
- The Ten Benefits of Favor
- Ten Signs of a Noble City
- And more…

To get your copy go to: https://destinybuilders.world/download-prayer/

ENDNOTES

[1] Margaret Mead, Robert B. Textor (2005). "The World Ahead: An Anthropologist Anticipates the Future", Berghahn Books, p.12

[2] Bounds, E.M., "The Complete Works of E. M. Bounds on Prayer: Experience the Wonders of God through Prayer", Baker Books, 2004

[3] Stanton, Andrew, "Democrat Calling for Trump to Be 'Eliminated' Sparks MAGA Fury," Newsweek, https://www.newsweek.com/dan-goldman-calling-trump-eliminated-sparks-maga-fury-1845364, Nov. 20, 2023, accessed Nov. 24 2023

[4] Meyer, Ken, 'I Take it Back': Joy Behar Made to Retract Comments, After Calling Trump a 'Domestic Terrorist,' Mediaite, https://www.mediaite.com/tv/i-take-it-back-joy-behar-made-to-retract-comments-after-calling-trump-a-domestic-terrorist/ June 11, 2020, Accessed November 24, 2023

[5] Thorton, Cedric "Big Ced", "Whoopi Goldberg Warns Trump: 'You're Not Gonna Run If You're In Jail'," Black Enterprise, https://www.blackenterprise.com/whoopi-goldberg-warns-president-trump-youre-not-gonna-run-if-youre-in-jail/, Dec 20, 2020, Accessed Nov 24, 2023

[6] Eady, Ashley, "15 Stars Who Imagined Violence Against Trump," The Wrap, August 15, 2018, https://www.thewrap.com/hollywood-stars-donald-trump-violent-death-kathy-griffin-snoop-dogg/ Accessed Nov. 24, 2023

[7] Upper III, George, "GOP Rep Stefanik Files Ethics Complaint Against Judge Engoron Alleging 'Bizarre Behavior' and Anti-Trump 'Bias,'" The Western Journal,

Nov. 10, 2023, https://www.westernjournal.com/gop-rep-stefanik-files-ethics-complaint-judge-engoron-alleging-bizarre-behavior-anti-trump-bias/ Accessed Nov. 27, 2023

[8] Knudsen, Hanna, "Exclusive — Trump Lawyer Alina Habba: NY Judge Was 'Definitely Assisting' Anti-Trump Lawyers," https://www.breitbart.com/politics/2023/11/07/exclusive-trump-lawyer-alina-habba-ny-judge-was-definitely-assisting-anti-trump-lawyers/, Nov 7, 2023, Accessed online Nov 24, 2023

[9] Robert F. Kennedy (1998). "Make Gentle the Life of the World: The Vision of Robert F. Kennedy", Harcourt

[10] Kaitlan Collins, Kevin Liptak, Katelyn Polantz, Sara Murray, Evan Perez, Gabby Orr and Dan Berman, "FBI Executes Search Warrant at Trump's Mar-a-Lago in Document Investigation," CNN Politics, https://www.cnn.com/2022/08/08/politics/mar-a-lago-search-warrant-fbi-donald-trump/index.html, August 9, 2022, Accessed Nov 24, 2023

[11] Goldman, Emma, "The Social Significance of the Modern Drama," 1914

[12] "Manipulus Florum". Book edited by Thomas Hibernicus

[13] Jackson, Andrew, Inspiring Quotes, https://www.inspiringquotes.us/quotes/PVcF_gjl1O2rw Accessed Nov 28, 2023

[14] Barton, David, "The Bulletproof George Washington," Wallbuilder Press, 2002

[15] Rand, Ayn, "The Virtue of Selfishness," Signet, 1964

[16] Twain, Mark, "The Bible According to Mark Twain," University of Georgia Press, 1995

[17] Dr. Martin Luther King, Jr. (2011). "Why We Can't Wait", Beacon Press, p.62

[18] Saint Augustine, Writings of Saint Augustine: The City of God, Image Publishing, 1958

[19] Taylor-Greene, Marjorie, Jan. 8, 2021, https://greene.house.gov/news/documentsingle.aspx?DocumentID=110 Accessed Nov 28, 2023

[20] "The Writings of George Washington: Being His Correspondence, Addresses, Messages, and Other Papers, Official and Private". https://www.azquotes.com/quote/307743 Accessed Nov 28, 2023

[21] Arendt, Hannah, The Origins of Totalitarianism, Harcourt, Brace, Jovanovich, 1973

[22] Acts 5

[23] Franklin, Benjamin, The Silence Dogwood Essays, 1722

[24] "Letter from Birmingham Jail," 16 Apr. 1963

[25] Speech on the twenty-fourth anniversary of emancipation in the District of Columbia, Washington, D.C., Apr. 1886

[26] Selassie, Haile, 1963 Address to a special session of the UN General Assembly, Oct. 4, making him the first head of state to address both that organization and the League of Nations

[27] Pride and Prejudice, chapter 31, http://www.literaturepage.com/read/prideandprejudice-156.html, Accessed Dec 3, 2023

[28] Farrand, Max, "The Records of the Federal Convention of 1787" 1911.

[29] Bounds, E.M., "The Complete Works of E. M. Bounds on Prayer: Experience the Wonders of God through Prayer", Baker Books, 2004

[30] Franklin, Benjamin at the Constitutional Convention, Liberty Fund Network, July 27, 2022, https://oll.libertyfund.org/reading-room/2022-07-27-benjamin-franklin-at-the-constitutional-convention. Accessed Dec 1, 2023.

About the Author

Karen Hardin is a writer, literary agent and cofounder of Destiny Builders, a nonprofit organization to the nations and to governmental leaders. She also leads the City-by-City Global Intercessory Prayer Network (city-by-city.org) and AwakeOklahoma.com with the goal to bring transformation and revival to our cities and nation.

She has been published in a number of publications including *USA Today, Western Journal, Intercessors for America, Charisma, Elijah List, CBN.com, American Faith*, and more.

She and her husband, Kevin, have worked extensively in Asia for thirty years. The last several years, Karen has been led to Washington, D.C., and the arena of government. She has spoken before the United Nations, participated in the National Prayer Breakfast and leads prayer tours in Washington, D.C. Her passion is to help raise up others to recognize and walk in their identity and destiny.

For additional information, go to destinybuilders.world or to sign up for her weekly prophetic insights blog go to: karenhardin.com.